D0118617

MOON

Alice Harman

WINDMILL
BOOKS
NEW YORK

Published in 2016 by **Windmill Books**, an Imprint of Rosen Publishing
29 East 21st Street, New York, NY 10010

Copyright © 2016 Wayland / Windmill

Editor: Alice Harman
Design: Rocket Design (East Anglia) Ltd
Other illustrations: Stefan Chabluk/Bill Donohue
Consultant: Kate Ruttle

Picture and illustration credits: Chabluk, Stefan: 8; Donohoe, William:
4–5; Dreamstime: Keifer 6, Clearviewstock 7, Mashka64 10l, Kenhurst 10r,
Ginesvalera 11: Morehead Planetarium and Science Center 21; NASA: 6 inset,
9, 13, 16, 17, 18, 19, 20; Shutterstock: Suppakij1017 4 inset, MichaelJung
12, Mr BenBa (chair) 12; Wikimedia: Dylan Kereluk 14/15, Wiki Commons/
Gregory H. Revera cover and title page.

Cataloging-in-Publication Data
Harman, Alice.
Moon / by Alice Harman.
p. cm. — (Fact finders: space)
Includes index.
ISBN 978-1-5081-9129-2 (pbk.)
ISBN 978-1-5081-9130-8 (6-pack)
ISBN 978-1-5081-9131-5 (library binding)
1. Moon — Juvenile literature. 1. Title.
QB582 H37 2016
523.3—d23

Manufactured in the United States of America
CPSIA Compliance Information: Batch #BW16PK: For Further Information contact
Rosen Publishing, New York, New York at 1-800-237-9932

FACT FINDER

There is a question for you
to answer on each spread
in this book. You can check
your answers on page 24.

CONTENTS

WHAT IS THE MOON?

A moon is an object, made of rock or **ice**, that moves around a **planet**. Our planet is called Earth. The Moon moves around, or **orbits**, Earth.

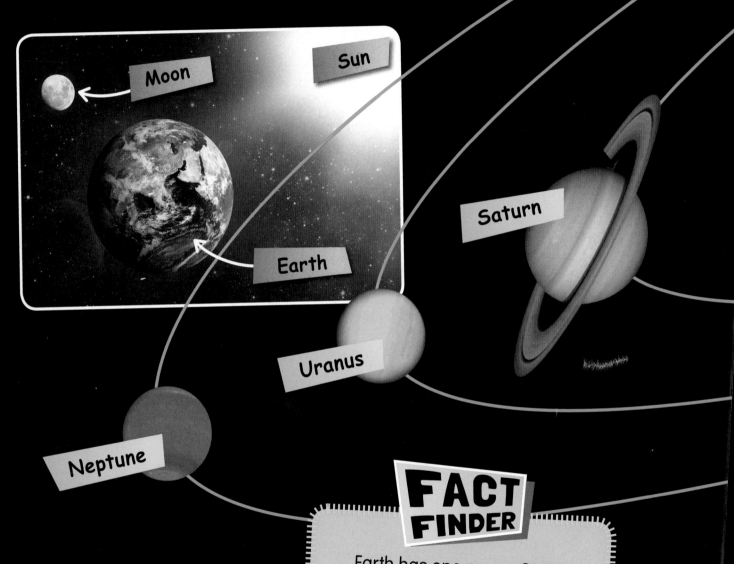

Moon

Sun

Earth

Saturn

Uranus

Neptune

FACT FINDER

Earth has one moon. Some planets have lots of moons. Mercury and Venus have no moons at all.

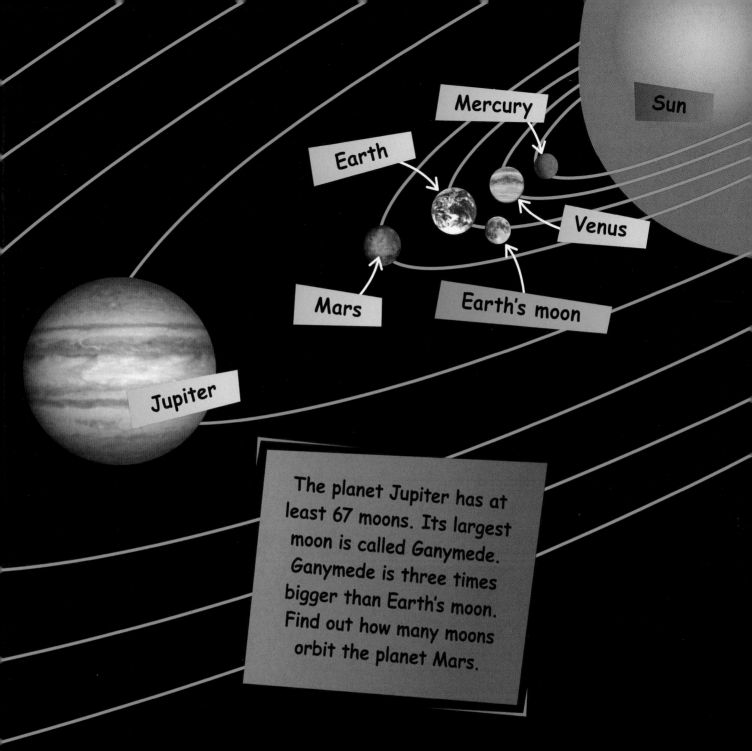

Earth

Mercury

Sun

Venus

Mars

Earth's moon

Jupiter

The planet Jupiter has at least 67 moons. Its largest moon is called Ganymede. Ganymede is three times bigger than Earth's moon. Find out how many moons orbit the planet Mars.

The Moon is more than 4 **billion** years old. It is around 100 **million** years younger than Earth. Scientists think that the Moon was formed when another planet crashed into Earth.

THE SURFACE OF THE MOON

maria

The Moon has dark patches called maria on its **surface**. The dark-colored rock in the maria is formed from **lava** that **erupted** from **volcanoes** a long time ago.

The surface of the Moon is covered in dust. There is no wind to blow the dust around. Find out how many years this man's footprint on the Moon could last.

The surface of the Moon looks smooth, but it is actually very rough and bumpy. It has many deep holes called craters in its surface.

The Moon's craters were formed when rocky objects called meteoroids and asteroids crashed into it. This happened 3 or 4 billion years ago.

FACT FINDER

The deepest crater on the Moon is the South Pole-Aitken Basin. The tallest mountain on Earth (Mount Everest) could fit inside this crater with only a bit of its top sticking out.

INSIDE THE MOON

The Moon is made up of three main layers. The **core** is at its center, the **mantle** surrounds the core, and the **crust** covers the mantle.

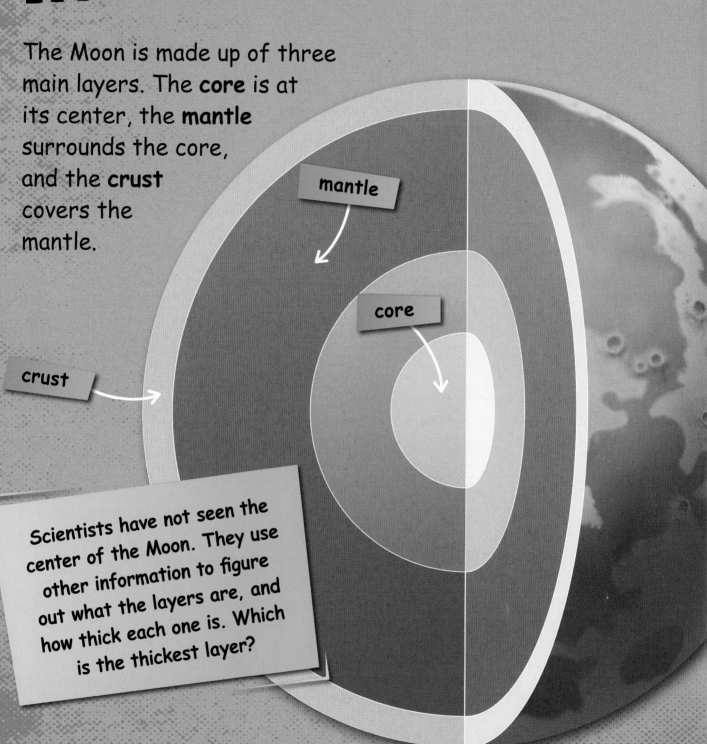

mantle

core

crust

Scientists have not seen the center of the Moon. They use other information to figure out what the layers are, and how thick each one is. Which is the thickest layer?

The crust and the mantle of the Moon are made of rock. The core is made of **metal**. Most of the Moon is **solid** but parts of the mantle and the core are **liquid**.

This machine feels movements deep under the Moon's surface. It gives scientists information about the Moon's liquid parts.

FACT FINDER

In 1988, people were asked what they thought the Moon was made of. More than 1 in 10 people said it was made of cheese!

THE MOON'S CYCLE

The Moon does not give out any light. We can only see the Moon when light from the Sun **bounces** off its surface. The Moon seems to shine brightly at night, but this light really comes from the Sun.

During the day, the Sun shines directly on Earth. This makes the sky brighter, so the Moon cannot be seen as clearly as at night.

day

night

FACT FINDER

The Moon is sometimes lit up by sunlight that bounces off Earth. This is called earthshine. However, this light is not very strong so we cannot normally see it.

new moon

crescent moon

half moon

full moon

As the Moon orbits Earth, the Sun shines on different parts of it. We only see the parts of the Moon that are lit up by the Sun. The Moon never changes shape, but it looks like it does.

The Moon's cycle is the time in which the Moon seems to get bigger and then smaller. Four stages of the cycle are shown here. Find out how many days the Moon's cycle lasts.

THE MOON AND EARTH

On Earth, we only ever see one side of the Moon. The Moon turns around once in the time it takes to orbit Earth once.

Imagine you are the Moon and a chair is Earth. Walk around the chair, turning so you always face it. Does your back ever face the chair?

The side of the Moon that we cannot see from Earth is called the far side of the Moon.

The other side of the Moon has maria and craters in different places. This means that it looks different from the side of the Moon we see from Earth.

Astronauts took this picture of the other side of the Moon when they were in space.

TIDES

The Moon orbits Earth because a pulling **force** called gravity holds it in place. Earth's gravity pulls on the Moon, and the Moon's gravity pulls Earth back.

The Moon's gravity pulls on the water in Earth's oceans. This makes the ocean water move back and forth. These movements are called tides.

At high tide, the water from the oceans moves further up onto the land. At low tide, it moves back and the land can be seen again.

Do you think this picture was taken at high tide or low tide?

FACT FINDER

Earth's gravity pulls at everything on Earth's surface, including you! If there was no gravity, we would float away from Earth into space.

THE MOON LANDING

The first **spacecraft** to land on the Moon's surface was called Apollo 11. It was an American spacecraft. It left Earth on July 16, 1969, and landed on the Moon three days later.

The **astronauts** in Apollo 11 were Neil Armstrong, Michael Collins and Buzz Aldrin. Who was the first man to ever walk on the Moon?

American flag

The Moon's gravity is very weak. This made it difficult for astronauts to walk around on the Moon.

FACT FINDER

The fastest speed reached by Apollo 11 was 24,450 mph (39,500 km/h). That is 40 times faster than the top speed of a large airplane.

The astronauts did scientific **experiments** on the Moon. They took away bits of rock and soil to learn more about them. They also left an American **flag** on the Moon.

EXPLORING THE MOON

Since the first Moon landing, other spacecraft have gone to the Moon to learn more about it. In 1999, a spacecraft called the Lunar Prospector orbited the Moon to see if there was any water there.

The Lunar Prospector found **evidence** that there might be frozen water on the Moon. Do you know another name for frozen water?

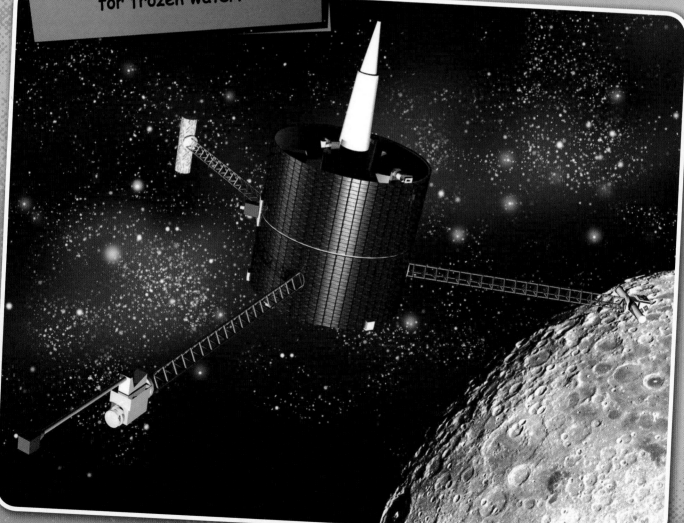

Astronauts wear **spacesuits** and carry big **tanks** of air when they are on the Moon. This is because people need to breathe air to stay alive, and there is no air on the Moon.

Astronauts can drive special cars called moon buggies when they are on the Moon. This helps them to explore the Moon's surface more quickly.

FACT FINDER

Dr. Eugene Shoemaker was a scientist who taught astronauts about moon craters. He always wanted to visit the Moon, but he couldn't go into space because of his health. After he died, his ashes were buried on the Moon.

COULD WE LIVE ON THE MOON?

Some scientists say that by 2024 astronauts will be able to live on the Moon for months at a time. The astronauts would stay in a small house that could be easily moved around.

This drawing shows the type of house that astronauts might live in on the Moon.

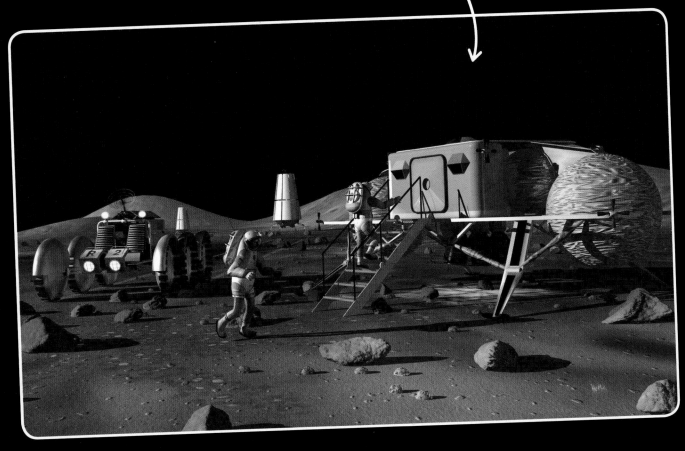

People need air, water and food to stay alive. None of these things are easily available on the Moon. However, there might be oxygen in the rock and frozen water deep underground. We could bring plants from Earth to grow food.

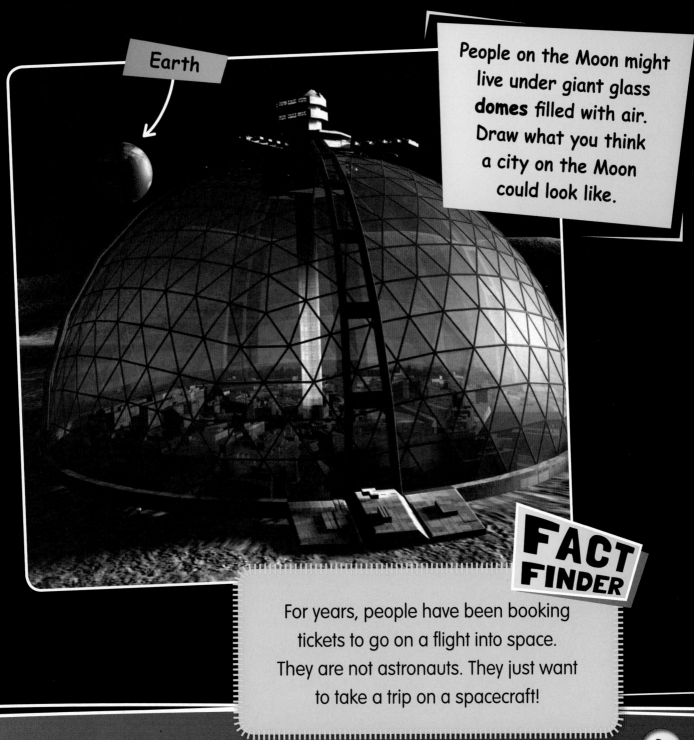

Earth

People on the Moon might live under giant glass **domes** filled with air. Draw what you think a city on the Moon could look like.

FACT FINDER

For years, people have been booking tickets to go on a flight into space. They are not astronauts. They just want to take a trip on a spacecraft!

QUIZ

Try to answer the questions below. Look back through the book to help you. Check your answers on page 24.

1 Does Earth move around the Moon?

a) yes
b) no

2 What is the Moon made of?

a) mostly rock, with some metal
b) mostly metal, with some rock
c) mostly cheese, with some rock

3 On Earth, we can only see one side of the Moon. True or not true?

a) true
b) not true

4 Does the Moon give out its own light?

a) yes
b) no

5 How often does the Moon change shape?

a) every day
b) every month
c) never

6 In what year was the first Moon landing?

a) 1899
b) 1969
c) 2009

GLOSSARY

astronaut person whose job is to travel and work in space

billion a thousand million (1,000,000,000)

bounce to move away in another direction after hitting something

core part at the center of a planet or moon

crust outside layer of a planet or moon

dome rounded building or top part of a building

erupt to burst out suddenly

evidence facts that show something is true

experiment test to try and find out information about something

flag piece of cloth with special colors and drawings that represents a country or organization

force power or energy that makes an object move or stop

ice frozen water

lava hot, melted rock that comes out of a volcano

liquid form of material that can flow and is wet, like water

mantle hot, partly liquid layer of rock below the top layer of a planet or moon

metal material that is normally hard and shiny, like gold

million a thousand thousands (1,000,000)

orbit when an object in space moves in a curved path around another object

planet large object in space that moves around a star

solid form of material that you can normally see and touch, like rock

spacecraft vehicle, like an airplane, that is used to travel in space

spacesuit special piece of clothing that completely surrounds a person so they can breathe air when they are in space

surface the top layer of an object

tank large container used to hold gas (like air) or liquid (like water)

volcano hill with a hole in its center, which liquid rock from underground can come out through

INDEX

ANSWERS

Pages 5–18

page 5: Mars has two known moons, Phobos and Deimos.

page 6: It could last for millions of years.

page 8: The diagram shows that the mantle is the thickest layer.

page 11: The Moon's cycle lasts 29.5 days, just a bit less than a normal month.

page 12: No, only your front should face the chair. In the same way, only one side of the Moon ever faces Earth.

page 15: This picture shows low tide. The water has moved back and the ground below can be seen.

page 16: Neil Armstrong

page 18: Another name for frozen water is ice.

Quiz answers

1   b) no
2   a) mostly rock, with some metal
3   a) true
4   b) no
5   c) never
6   b) 1969